Made in United States
Troutdale, OR
09/23/2025

34802065R00090